PORTRAIT OF THE
SUSSEX COAST

THE COLOUR AND SPIRIT OF
SUSSEX BY THE SEA

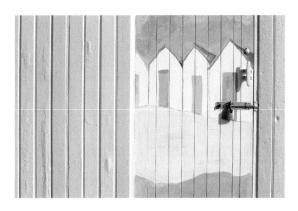

IAIN McGOWAN

HALSGROVE

First published in Great Britain in 2008

Title page photograph: *Beach hut painting, Aldwick*

British Library Cataloguing-in-Publication Data
A CIP record for this title is available from the British Library

ISBN 978 1 84114 727 7

HALSGROVE
Halsgrove House
Ryelands Industrial Estate
Bagley Road, Wellington,
Somerset TA21 9PZ
Tel: 01823 653777
Fax: 01823 216796
email: sales@halsgrove.com
website: www.halsgrove.com

Printed and bound by D'Auria Industrie Grafiche, Italy

CONTENTS

INTRODUCTION

The Sussex coast stretches westwards along the English Channel from the Kent boundary near Camber Sands to Thorney Island within Chichester Harbour and its watery border with Hampshire. Despite the popular perception that much of this shoreline of some 150km has over the last one-hundred years become entirely engulfed by the spread of maritime suburbia, the Sussex coast in fact contains some of the finest seascapes in Southern England. Notable features are the magnificent white chalk cliffs of Beachy Head and the Seven Sisters – symbolic of England throughout much of the world – the glorious often deserted sandy beaches of Camber and the Witterings, the lonely, haunting hinterland of Pagham Harbour and the East Guldeford levels and the vegetated shingle of Lancing and Pett. Chichester Harbour has become a yachtsman's and ornithologist's paradise and it is this variety together with the elegant stuccoed terraces of Brighton and Hove, the castles of Arundel and Pevensey, the cobbled streets of Rye or the Saxon and Norman church masterpieces of Bishopstone, Bosham and Shoreham that make the Sussex coast such a fascinating area to visit.

Throughout its long history, Sussex has always looked out to and depended upon the sea and to this day the county is still possibly best known for its string of coastal resorts and towns that in many ways have become a part of our language and national institutions. However, as history and surviving antique maps will tell, the sea has not always been so kind and accommodating. It was the sea that allowed the Romans to land on these shores followed by the Saxons, Viking raiders and, of course, the Normans in 1066. Only since the early years of the eighteenth century when sea bathing became firstly a curative and then fashionable pastime has the coastline's resort status been developed. Up to this time, by constantly advancing and receding, the sea was as great an enemy as any invading force. Old Winchelsea was destroyed, Pevensey and Rye were left to decline and St Wilfred's monastery and cathedral at Selsey now lie under the sea. Elsewhere the course of both the Adur and Ouse altered over the centuries with dramatic effect upon Shoreham and Seaford. Brighthelmstone (later Brighton) was almost wiped out whilst numerous coastal lanes and byways between Worthing and Bognor Regis still align themselves mysteriously to the drowned communities of long ago. Severe coastal erosion has been and will continue to be a constant threat for generations to come.

Doctor Richard Russell published his famous treatise *Dissertation concerning the use of seawater in diseases of the glands* in1752 and it was this, together with the later arrival of the railways from the 1840s, that led directly to the establishment of much of the Sussex coast as the sought-after destination that we know today. Brighton, patronised by the Prince Regent developed to become the premier seaside resort in Britain followed to varying degrees by Bexhill, Bognor Regis, Eastbourne, Hastings, Littlehampton and Worthing. As the old traditional fishing industries slowly declined, the influx, first of wealthy visitors and then day-trippers amounted to a rebirth of the coast's fortunes.

Apart from the extraordinary visual and social variety offered by this coastline, another reason for its popularity is the weather and in particular the degree of sustained sunshine. Mainly sandwiched between the southern slopes of the South Downs and the sea, many of the coastal villages and resorts enjoy a unique micro-climate where the recorded hours of sunshine are some of the highest in Britain, often equalling those found further south in parts of Europe. It is this striking element of sunshine coupled with its geographical location and history that gives the Sussex coast much of its outstanding colour, mood and spirit. These are the factors that this book seeks to illustrate in a journey from Camber to Thorney and its associated hinterland, a place of warmth in every sense of the word, one of the country's most popular seaside destinations, Sussex by the Sea.

MAP OF THE SUSSEX COAST

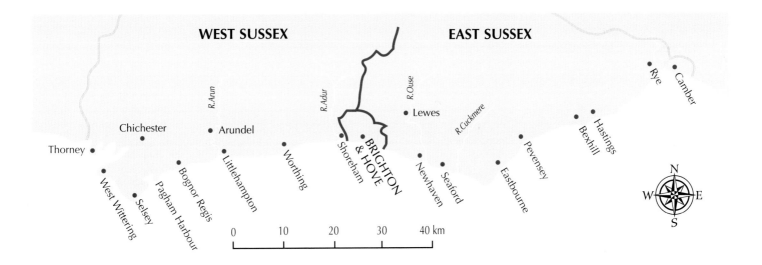

A glorious early summer's morning at Camber Sands. Stretching almost from the Kent boundary to Rye Harbour, this is the largest open sand beach in Sussex. Backed in places by high dunes, the sands are over 1km broad at low tide – a paradise for sand-castles, paddling and sun bathing. The village of Camber by contrast has been described as 'a haphazard collection of bungalows, shacks and shanties'. The name Camber was originally attributed to the shallow estuary that once served Old Winchelsea and Rye before the sea receded to leave the rich reclaimed grasslands to be found today.

CAMBER to PEVENSEY

Crude seafront advertising at Camber.

Travelling from Lydd in Kent along the coast road one enters East Sussex amongst a landscape of windswept open farmland and marsh, vegetated shingle, scattered cottages, numerous overhead power and service lines, barbed wire and semi-disused military ranges. In winter the area can be bleak in the extreme! Camber is soon reached to be followed by the timeless beauty of Rye and Winchelsea, the sandstone cliffs of Fairlight, a busy Hastings conurbation, Bexhill, Norman's Bay and historic Pevensey. In this first part of a coastal journey, the contrast and variation of interest soon becomes apparent

The Church of St Mary, East Guldeford. Between Camber and Rye, the East Guldeford Levels, reclaimed from the sea in the fifteenth century, extend north across the county boundary into Romney Marsh. The hamlet of East Guldeford and its church lie isolated surrounded by far-reaching grassland, drainage ditches and wide open skies. The church itself is unusual with its brick construction and hipped twin roof and dates from the very early sixteenth century.

A view over the Rother Levels near Iden looking towards the Kent border and the Isle of Oxney. It is hard to believe that much of this land was at one time submerged by the sea providing access for ships using the numerous, now inland, wharves and quays accessible in present times only by small craft up narrow often shallow channels and the upper reaches of the various rivers. A glance at a modern day map and the instances of the words 'wharf' and 'ferry' give immediate clues to the history of this area.

Rye Harbour. The community of Rye Harbour is separated from the town of Rye itself and is situated out near the mouth of the River Rother on the marsh and shingle. Consisting of a scattering of sheds, old and new cottages, caravans, pubs and quays, it has a distinctive character all of its own. Much of the surrounding land with its gravel pits and lagoons has now become part of the Rye Harbour Nature Reserve, a Site of Special Scientific Interest and regarded as one of the finest examples of shingle vegetation in Britain. The area is also used as a safe haven and stopover for many shore and nesting birds. Due to sea movement and changes, some 55,000 tons of shingle are still dredged each year to enable the harbour to be kept in use.

Situated within the peaceful churchyard of Rye Harbour's Church of the Holy Spirit is this memorial to the crew of the lifeboat *Mary Stanford*. The boat set out in stormy weather on 15 November 1928 to the rescue of a Latvian steamer damaged by a collision off Dungeness. Despite the steamer's crew being taken off by the other vessel, the message was sent too late for the lifeboat crew, all seventeen of whom were lost when the lifeboat capsized in the overpowering seas. A lifeboat station still operates from Rye Harbour and a board on the nearby 'watch house' records many rescues carried out over the years.

Church Square, Rye. The historic town of Rye, originally founded in the eleventh century, was built on a small island close to the sea, but as the sea receded, it has been left stranded almost 5km inland on a sandstone hill surrounded by the flat fertile marshland. As one of the ancient Cinque Ports, it once had a busy harbour and despite frequent attacks by the French during the fourteenth and fifteenth centuries, the town retained much of its prosperity, recognised by the title 'Rye Royal' bestowed upon it by Queen Elizabeth in 1573. As the sea began to retreat, the harbour slowly silted up to leave the town almost frozen in time clustered around its unique hilltop site with St Mary's Church at its apex. With its outstanding variety of closely-packed period buildings lining the often steep and narrow cobbled streets, the town's rich history is still very much in evidence and in the words of Arthur Mee 'is like no other town in England'. Today its once bustling quaysides echo to the sound of pleasure boats cruising along the River Rother and the footsteps of the many visitors from whom much of its income is now derived.

Crowds watch a re-enactment entitled the 'Seige of Rye' organised by the Order of Rye Longbowmen as part of the Rye Medieval Festival. Archery, jousting and cannon volley demonstrations are all featured in this popular event together with Eagle and Vulture displays and a concert celebrating medieval music and dance. In 1295 King Edward I amassed some 25,000 archers outside the town as part of his plans for a national army.

Camber Castle was built by Henry VIII as part of a coastal defence system formed of a chain of forts against possible invasion from France. It was completed to a polygonal design in 1544 and situated on a shingle ridge overlooking the shallow harbour that then existed between Rye and Winchelsea. However, due to the rapidly changing coastline and a build-up of shingle, the castle was abandoned in 1642 and its ruin now stands in solitary isolation almost 2 km from the shore.

Opposite: The Royal Military Canal near Winchelsea. This peaceful scene at Pett Level shows part of what was then the Sussex section of the Royal Military Canal. The canal, simply a wide dyke was dug in 1804 as a defence barrier in response to suspicions of Napoleon. Routed principally around the north and west of Romney Marsh, the canal started at Cliff End near Pett reaching the Kent boundary at Iden and continuing on to Shorncliffe in Kent itself, a distance of some 45 km. Gun turrets intended along its banks were never constructed.

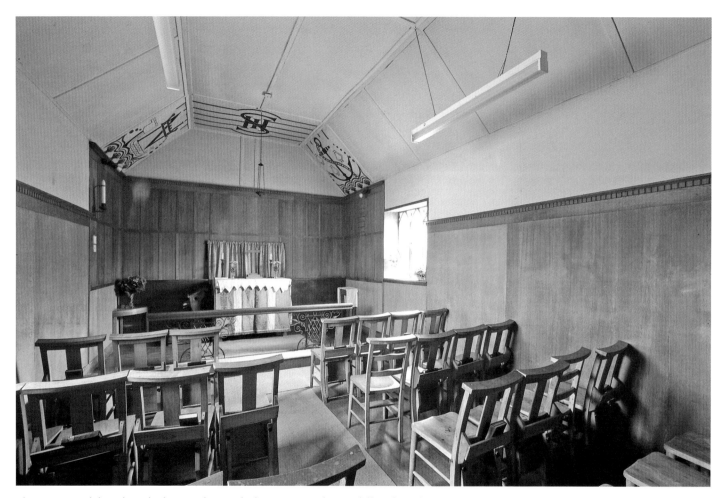

The interior of the Chapel of Ease of St Nicholas, Pett Level. At Cliff End, with the Pett Levels behind, this tiny chapel is built on the very fringes of the shingle stretching away eastwards to Winchelsea Beach. Dedicated to St Nicholas, the patron saint of sailors and children in 1935, the building was originally owned by the Admiralty and known as 'Rocket House' due to its former use by the coastguards to house equipment such as life-saving rocket apparatus. Closed during the Second World War, St Nicholas as the Chapel of Ease to St Mary and St Peter at Pett village has hosted regular Holy Communion services ever since. Overlooking the sea, the minute chapel's unpretentious exterior belies a simple uncluttered interior with a feeling of sincerity often found lacking in larger establishments elsewhere.

Sea defences, Winchelsea Beach. With continuing sea level changes and tidal flows, much of the 4km shingle beach between Cliff End and the village of Winchelsea Beach is heavily reinforced with rows of breakwaters and lines of timber groynes to prevent further coastal movement. Near the village the site of Rye New Harbour can still be seen, now a playing field, with the foundation stones of the two harbour arms much in evidence on the beach at low tide. Completed in July 1787 the harbour was abandoned later the same year due to excessive shingle build up at its entrance. The project had taken 63 years to build, seven Acts of Parliament and at a cost of some £200,000 at eighteenth century values!

The original town of Winchelsea was destroyed by the sea's encroachment particularly after the great storm of 1287. Due to its strategic importance a new town was laid out on a raised promontory to the north of the old site under the direction of Edward I. The town was planned in the form of a rigid grid of streets and occupied from the late thirteenth century onwards only to subsequently suffer the same fate as Rye with numerous French attacks and a retreating coast-line. From the end of the fifteenth century, despite its ambitious scale, the partly built town simply shrank back into the spacious, attractive, somewhat nostalgic village to be seen today some 3km inland from the present shoreline.

From Cliff End, the land rises rapidly to Fairlight, later dropping after some 10km to Hastings. As the Wealden clays reach the sea, the dramatic sandstone cliffs rise to over 100m near Fairlight Glen, an outstanding location to study the geological evolution of the Weald. The photograph shows typical cliff formation and strata near Cliff End.

Opposite: The view on a clear day looking back eastwards from near Fairlight towards Winchelsea Beach and in the very far distance Dungeness in Kent. Fairlight Church 170m above sea level acts as a landmark for many miles and particularly for mariners up and down the Channel.

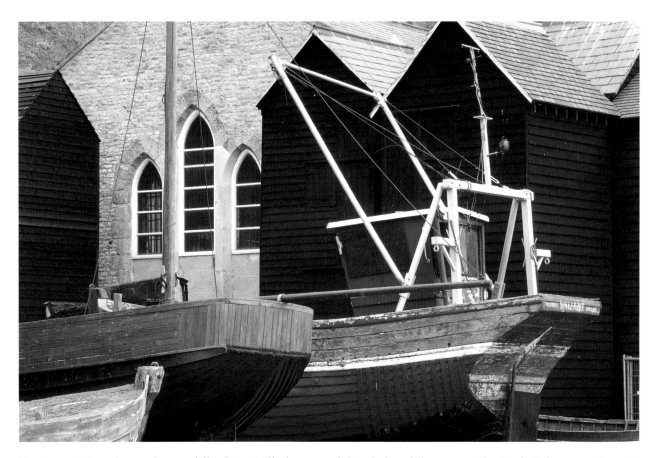

Hastings. Below the sandstone cliffs of East Hill, the area of shingle beach known as The Stade is home to Europe's largest fleet of beach-launched fishing boats. The word 'stade' meaning 'landing place' reflects Hastings history as a maritime centre for over a thousand years and as one of the principal Cinque Ports. The Cinque Ports were a confederation of certain Sussex and Kentish coastal towns that obtained privileges from the monarchy in early medieval times in exchange for supplying ships for the nation's defence. In the case of Hastings, the fishermen were given free use of The Stade, a right still strongly defended today. One of the principal features of the area are the tall, thin, weatherboarded and gable-roofed net shops clustered along the beach. These distinctive structures, possibly originating from Tudor times, are almost unique to Hastings and used for storage of fishermen's tackle and nets. *(Above)* A typical Stade scene. The stone building, formerly a church, is now the Fishermen's Museum.

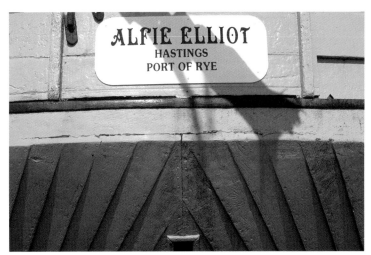

Evidence of The Stade's fishing connections.

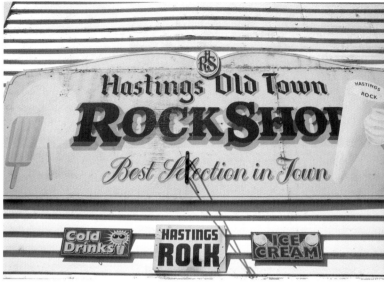

Evidence of a different culture at Hastings and for those with a sweet tooth!

Hastings' East Hill lift is the steepest funicular railway in Britain. Built in 1902 and originally water powered it ascends from The Stade up through a rock cutting in the cliff wall to the hill's summit providing spectacular views to below and over Hastings old town. A similar railway also operates at the adjacent West Hill giving easy access to the remaining fragments of William the Conqueror's Hastings Castle built shortly after 1069.

The striking temple-like portico of the Church of St Mary-in-the-Castle situated at the centre of Pelham Crescent overlooking the sea. The crescent is possibly the most impressive of the Regency additions to the old town set immediately below and in places cut into the cliffs, but sadly is not in the best of condition. The church itself built in 1828 was so named due to it replacing the ruined collegiate church within the castle on the hills above.

Opposite: Old Town, Hastings. The historic old town, nestling between the two ridges of East and West Hills and stretching down to the sea dates back to the fourteenth century replacing earlier communities sacked by the French. It is a fascinating contrast to what is principally a Victorian resort with a few Regency survivals. Consisting of the parallel High Street and All Saints Street, reached and linked by numerous narrow lanes, winding passages and alley-ways, the old town presents a remarkable variety of almost unspoilt domestic architecture from different periods and styles. From the hills above, the colours and forms of the crowded roofs take on a patchwork appearance, whilst on a fine summer's day a certain continental atmosphere can prevail.

Victorian terracing, Bexhill-on-Sea. Bexhill-on-Sea was promoted by the De la Warr family as late as the 1880s as a select up-market seaside resort adjacent to the inland older village of Bexhill itself with its church dating back to Saxon times and period weatherboarded cottages. The resort not only has a certain Edwardian character still prevalent today but is renowned as the birthplace of British motor racing and as the first resort to permit mixed sea bathing. Its wide seafront promenade, where motor racing was once staged, and cliff top walks extend for 8km from the outskirts of Hastings at historic Bulverhythe to Cooden adjoining Norman's Bay.

Colourful beach huts near Bulverhythe. Once an ancient port between Bexhill and St Leonards, little now remains of Bulverhythe apart from fragments of a medieval chapel and the remorseless engulfing by Hastings maritime suburbia. *(Right)* The rhythmical colours of beach changing facilities at Bexhill.

The De la Warr Pavilion is undoubtedly Bexhill's best known building. Designed by the architects Eric Mendelsohn and Serge Chermayeff and completed in 1935, the concrete and steel pavilion is now regarded as one of the finest and most stylish international modernist movement buildings of any size in Britain. With its angular solid walling, continuous glazing and projecting semi-circular staircase wings, the pavilion stands elevated above the shore dominating the domed colonnade below. Used for a variety of purposes over the years, the Grade I listed pavilion has recently undergone a multi-million pound refurbishment where its gloriously open galleries, theatre, conference facilities, terraces and restaurant are once more the subject of considerable interest and support. *(Above)* The south staircase wing and part of the seafront elevation. *(Opposite)* Two views of the Art Deco lighting and sweeping stair within the south staircase wing.

Norman's Bay. The predominantly low-lying coasts of East Sussex have always been an ideal landing area for any invading forces. As a result a series of forty-six circular brick fortifications known as Martello Towers were built between Eastbourne and Rye Harbour between 1805 and 1810 as a defence against a feared Napoleonic attack. The towers, with walls up to 2m thick and with doors high above ground level, had a main gun mounted on the roof. They were sited at the back of beaches where landings seemed likely. Now, many have been demolished or washed away but ten still remain and this view of Norman's Bay shows one of the towers with Eastbourne in the far distance. The name 'Martello' was derived from a similar structure that opposed British landings in Corsica during the late eighteenth century. A further tower was later built at Seaford and is in use as a museum.

Roman walling, Pevensey Castle. A castle was built here in about 1100 shortly after the Norman invasion and within the walls of the third-century Roman fort of Anderida; a reminder of Pevensey's importance as a Cinque Port in medieval times long before the sea retreated over 2km to the south. Most of the Roman walls, described as the finest Roman monument in Sussex and enclosing an area of some 4ha, still stand and it was within these that William the Conqueror and his army spent their first night on English soil prior to the fateful battle of 1066.

An ethereal sense of space and colour hangs over Eastbourne's empty beaches and promenade on an early spring day viewed from the pier. For many the town is regarded as one of the finest seaside resorts in Southern England with holiday visitors to be found from all over the country. As late as 1813 Eastbourne was noted as a small fashionable bathing place and it was not until the 1850s, on the initiative of the 7th Duke of Devonshire, that major development began. With safe sands, a Victorian pier and flower-lined promenade backed by landscaped gardens, elegant hotels and large private houses, this distinguished town soon became affectionately known as 'Empress of the Watering Places'.

EASTBOURNE to ROTTINGDEAN

A sea fret rolls in over the beaches to soften the outline of Eastbourne's pier on an early summer's morning.

The coastline from Eastbourne to Rottingdean not only includes the resorts of Eastbourne and Seaford and the port of Newhaven but above all is a coast of predominantly chalk cliffs. As the rolling South Downs meet the sea, literally at the western end of Eastbourne's promenade, the cliffs rise as an undulating dazzling white wall of exposed precipitous chalk. Beachy Head, the Seven Sisters, Cuckmere Haven, Seaford Head and Telscombe Cliffs – these are some of the most iconic scenes not only of Sussex but of England itself. This is a seascape that has inspired numerous writers and artists over the centuries and one that can still arouse that certain indomitable spirit in emotional chorus when we sing of William Blake's England's Mountains Green.

Now in the care of the Langham Hotel, this beautifully restored bathing machine is one of only a few surviving machines remaining from the many thousands once to be found on the beaches of the Sussex resorts. Simply a decorated wooden hut on wheels and with stairs at both ends, the machine enabled prospective bathers to enter at one end from the beach, undress in total privacy and then descend into the water from the other end, sometimes with assistance if required. The machines were moved up or down the beaches according to the tides and were one of the factors that helped encourage sea bathing during the first half of the eighteenth century.

Eastbourne's 5km promenade is particularly noted for its floral displays throughout the year. In places the promenade comprises three different levels between which the sloping banks and beds are often carpeted in colour interspersed by numerous seats and benches allowing visitors to savour the scene. With its outstanding recorded hours of sunshine the resort can easily start to take on a Mediterranean character in high summer.

The seafront open-air bandstand concerts are one of the most popular attractions of the resort, with performances almost daily over the summer months by various local and visiting brass and concert bands. Special events such as Rock 'n Roll nights, Prom's nights, firework concerts, Big Band nights and Gilbert and Sullivan nights are also featured in the season's comprehensive programme. The Art-Deco bandstand, completed in 1935, is noted for the excellence of its acoustics.

Eastbourne's pier at dusk. The 300m pier, designed by Eugenius Birch, was opened in 1872 and is unique in featuring a rare Camera Obscura under one of its domes. The revolving camera shows panoramic views of the surrounding scene projected by natural light via a mirror and lens on to a circular screen and is still open for viewing by the general public. Due to storm damage in the late nineteenth century, part of the pier was rebuilt requiring a ramp at the change of levels partway along the structure.

Beachy Head at 163m is the highest chalk cliff on the south coast being particularly well-known due to its close proximity to Eastbourne and the eye catching red and white lighthouse below. As such the scene has become one of the classic landmarks of Great Britain. The light house, completed in 1902, was the third to be built replacing the former Belle Tout lighthouse, now a private residence, on top of the cliffs and its predecessor dating back to 1828. Most of the labour and materials required for the present structure were lowered via an aerial ropeway from the cliff's summit. Despite its small appearance when viewed from above, the lighthouse is some 45m high, its beam being discernible over a distance of 50km.

Amongst this magnificent scenery it is regrettable that Beachy Head has also acquired an unwelcome notoriety as a popular location for suicide. On average at least one person a month has leapt to a certain death from the high cliffs which in many places bear tragic memorials, as shown here, to such wasted lives. Prominent notices by the Samaritans and regular day and evening patrols by landscape workers and a chaplaincy team are an attempt to halt this death rate.

West of Beachy Head, the precipitous chalk cliffs continue for some 11km to Cuckmere Haven. Known as the Seven Sisters they form one of the most dramatic and celebrated sections of coastal scenery in England. Along their undulating tops the popular South Downs Way long distance bridle path starts its journey from Eastbourne to Winchester. The photograph shows the cliffs viewed from near Cuckmere Haven in stormy conditions.

Opposite: The Seven Sisters from below Birling Gap at low tide. Birling Gap offers the only means of access to the beaches below the cliffs via a stepped walkway above which a hotel and a few houses brave the constantly receding friable chalk face crumbling at a rate of over ½m each year. Cliff falls are common especially after sharp frosts or winter storms.

A last glimpse eastwards from above Seaford Head towards the Seven Sisters in wintry late afternoon light. From here almost the entire range of cliffs can be seen from Haven Brow along to Went Hill Brow with the old Belle Tout lighthouse in the far distance. Beyond the foreground headlands the winding River Cuckmere reaches the sea at the spectacular flood plain of Cuckmere Haven, one of the few undeveloped estuaries remaining along the south coast and now incorporated within the Seven Sisters Country Park.

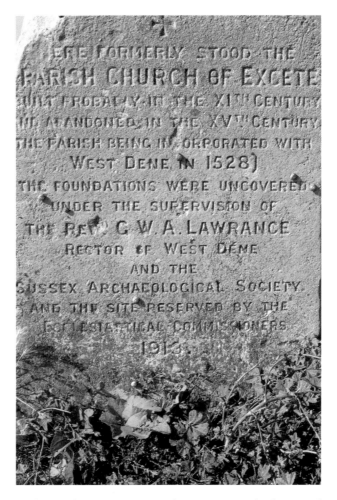

High on the Downs overlooking the Cuckmere estuary a solitary stone marks the site of Excete church. Once a small fishing village Exceat, as it is now spelt, was lost due to the Black Death of 1348 and repeated incursions by French raiders. It finally became a part of Westdean parish and the only reminders of a once thriving community are a single farm and the grass-covered church foundations.

On the western side of the Cuckmere Valley near Cuckmere Haven the hill known as High and Over has become a popular location for parascending as shown here. The river can be seen in the valley on its sinuous course from Alfriston to the sea.

Almost opposite High and Over on the east bank of the river the attractive small village of Litlington still features the Litlington Tea Gardens dating back to the nineteenth century and claimed to be the oldest tea gardens in Sussex. In an age of fast food it is a pleasure to pause here in the often sunny gardens and to appreciate that such leisurely places still exist in an increasingly frenetic world.

Beyond Cuckmere Haven and the Seven Sisters Country Park the chalk cliffs rise briefly at Seaford Head before the land descends to the town itself. The photograph shows the view from the eastern extremity of Seaford's promenade looking over the very necessary sea defences towards the head and with the remains of old fortifications above.

Part of the flint tower of Seaford's substantial Norman Church of St Leonard. Seaford at one time was an important Norman harbour and later one of the Cinque Ports and the size of its parish church reflect the town's past glories. Its prosperity continued until the fourteenth century after which a combination of the Black Death, French raiders and a diversion of its sea trade to nearby Newhaven, arising from the changing course of the River Ouse due to storms in the sixteenth century, pushed Seaford in to a steady decline. Today little remains of the old town and the new resort has grown up in a notably piece-meal fashion without much evidence of guidance or control.

In recent years Seaford's promenade has been considerably improved and updated and rows of new beach huts add a colourful aspect to the maritime scene.

Opposite: A wintry late afternoon view along Seaford's modest promenade towards distant Newhaven and the cliffs beyond. The final Martello Tower, constructed in 1810, is on the right and is now used as a museum.

The changing course of the River Ouse from its mouth at Seaford prior to the storms of 1579, to nearer Newhaven not only left Seaford in a state of decay but also created a dry depression along the course of the old river bed running parallel to the coastline. In 1762 tidal mills were first constructed using this old water course as tidal storage ponds on a site approximately mid-way between Seaford and Newhaven, the resulting community becoming known as Tide Mills. The mills were able to use tidal energy for about sixteen hours each day and continued to operate until closure late in the nineteenth century. Today nothing remains of this once bustling but isolated community apart from scattered flint and brick walling amongst the desolate shingle landscape. The photograph shows the view over the old river's watercourse looking towards Denton on the edge of the Downs behind Newhaven.

Remaining fragments of brick walling at Tide Mills close to the old tidal dam with its wheel tunnels and sluice gates. Not far from this site a Chailey Heritage Marine Hospital was built in 1924 for boys with physical disabilities recovering from operations. This too has since been demolished leaving a rash of old concrete foundations and brick piers facing the sea.

Behind Tide Mills and less than 2km from the coast, in a hollow at the edge of the Downs, lies the once small hamlet of Bishopstone now only separated from Seaford's encroaching urban development by just a few fields and hedgerows. Here the Saxon Church of St Andrew is remarkable for its beauty and for the degree of pre-conquest construction still remaining. The nave and what is now the porch, but was once a side chapel, are both of Saxon origin, the latter unusually featuring a sundial over its entrance incised with a cross and the word 'Eadric' as shown here. The sundial also indicated the four Saxon 'tides' of the day each being divided into three parts.

Opposite: Storm clouds over the Downs near Denton. Between Bishopstone and Denton the South Downs rise from the coastal pastures upwards to their main ridge at Firle Beacon. Denton on the east bank of the River Ouse, opposite Newhaven, was once a small downland hamlet with just a country church, manor house and a few flint cottages but together with neighbouring South Heighton has now become engulfed by suburban housing speading out from the nearby town.

Newhaven. Once a small fishing community known as Meeching prior to the sixteenth-century storms, the village started to grow as a town following the formation of the new outlet to the sea by the River Ouse and its desertion of Seaford. Accordingly Meeching became Newhaven. Despite the intervening centuries there is little in the town of any antiquity, Newhaven having grown to become a cross-channel continental ferry port promoted during the mid nine-teenth century with the arrival of the railway. By the end of the same century most of the harbour as seen today had been constructed including a massive 1000m western breakwater all overlooked by the Palmerston-era Newhaven Fort completed in 1871. The River Ouse, some 60km long, drains much of the southern flank of Ashdown Forest and the Weald and as such was an important waterway for carrying products of the once prosperous Sussex iron industry.

Aspects of Newhaven. *(Top left)* Part of the nineteenth century fortifications below west cliff. *(Top right)* A weatherboarded light hut at the side of the harbour entrance dating back to the 1890s. *(Bottom right)* The gated entrance to the western breakwater. *(Bottom left)* Colour at Fanny Lulu's!

Peacehaven. Travelling west from Newhaven towards Brighton, the almost continual urban sprawl of Peacehaven, Telscombe Cliffs, Saltdean and in parts Rottingdean has done little to enhance either the Downland scenery or its coastal cliffs. Peacehaven was laid out after the great war uniquely on the zero degree longitude meridian line to a grid plan with promises of 'an attractive seaside garden city'. Alas the entire section of the coast above the cliffs has instead developed into what has been described as 'a kind of seaside slum' in many places 'a hopelessly ugly agglomeration of mean, squat bungalows'! *(Left)* One of the period, illustrated obelisks at the approaches to Peacehaven showing the cliffs and Meridian Monument. *(Below)* A grid plan 'avenue' typical of many to be found at Peacehaven.

In complete contrast to the urban development above, the undercliff walk commencing at Peacehaven and extending some 11km to Brighton's Black Rock is an outstanding and exhilarating addition to the coastline. Designed to combine a promenade with sea defences protecting and stabilising the base of the cliffs, the walk provides a spectacular coastal feature for walkers and cyclists. In places the stepped access from the cliff tops to the walk below has necessitated considerable cutting back of the chalk face to resemble vast, almost theatrical, stage settings as shown here at the eastern extremity of the walk.

Sunlight on the Saltdean Lido. Saltdean was never strictly a village: for centuries it was an open area of Downland with a few isolated cottages and farms. Following the example of Peacehaven, development began in the 1920s and by 1928 the western area of what was then the Saltdean Estate was incorporated as part of the parish of Rottingdean into the County Borough of Brighton. The Saltdean Lido was opened by the estate company in 1937 shortly after Rottingdean and Brighton's Black Rock pools in a period when open air swimming was in vogue. The lido was designed in an Art Deco curvilinear style and is now listed as a building of special architectural interest.

Opposite: A view along the undercliff walk from near Peacehaven looking east towards distant Seaford Head.

One of the seven sets of stained glass windows in the Church of St Margaret at Rottingdean made by William Morris from the designs of Sir Edward Burne-Jones. These beautifully coloured windows are often regarded as some of the finest work these two famous artists produced together. Sir Edward Burne-Jones lived in Rottingdean from 1880 until his death in 1898, his nephew Rudyard Kipling also living in the village before moving to Batemans at Burwash.

The view west from Rottingdean's cliffs towards the Brighton Marina and the City of Brighton & Hove itself, with the undercliff walk below. Just visible on the rocks near the sea's edge are the two lines of concrete blocks that once acted as foundations for the 6km 'Daddy Long Legs' Rottingdean Railway. The blocks held rails on which an electrically powered car with stilt-like legs and capable of seating 150 passengers ran from Black Rock to Rottingdean. Designed by Magnus Volk the railway opened in 1896 only to close some five years later due to the excessive maintenance difficulties and storm damage to the often submerged tracks and running gear.

Sussex by the Sea. The very epitome of the county's resort status as sunbathers enjoy the beach at Brighton on a hot summer's day. This view looks east from Brighton Pier towards the marina and in the far distance the white chalk cliffs of Telscombe and Rottingdean.

BRIGHTON to SHOREHAM

The interior of the Brighton Fishing Museum situated under the arches of the seafront's lower promenade.

The City of Brighton & Hove extends for over 15km along the coast from Saltdean in the east to Hove Lagoon, with a further 7km westwards into West Sussex to include Shoreham-by-Sea. Queen of the South, City by the Sea, even San Francisco in Sussex – just a few of the many epithets to describe what is generally regarded as the premier seaside resort in Britain made up of the twin towns of Brighton and Hove. In just over 250 years the community has grown from the 'poor and decayed' fishing village of Brighthelmstone to city status, a population well in excess of a quarter of a million and with an almost unique colourful, cosmopolitan character and flourishing cultural life. For many the city is quite literally 'the place to live' in every aspect.

Font detail, the Church of St Nicholas of Myra, Brighton. Brighthelmstone was probably in existence during Saxon times, the old town slowly evolving as a fishing and farming community. For a period, despite numerous French incursions, its prosperity gradually increased until the mid seventeenth century when further attacks, storm damage, subsequent erosion and a reduction of fish stocks started a steady decline leading to a halving of its population by the early 1700s and Defoe's description of it as 'a poor fishing town'. In the first of the series of French raids of 1514, the entire medieval town was torched only to be quickly rebuilt, the one surviving building being the parish church of St Nicholas of Myra which still stands today albeit it in a considerably enlarged condition. It is therefore possibly the oldest of Brighton's buildings, its chief treasure being the magnificent twelfth-century drum-shaped font often described as the finest piece of Norman carving in Sussex.

The Royal Pavilion, Brighton. With a rise in the fashion of sea bathing from the early eighteenth century and a new appreciation of the sea's curative and restorative powers, Brighthelmstone's fortunes began to improve dramatically and by the 1780s was becoming established as the country's leading coastal resort. It was during this period that the town was first visited by George, Prince of Wales, subsequently to become Prince Regent and later King George IV, and it was he who over a period of time transformed his modest seaside residence into the grand palace known today as the Royal Pavilion completed in 1822. With its pagoda roofs, minarets, colonnades and onion-shaped domes this oriental extravagance is undoubtedly Brighton's best known building and one of the most recognisable profiles in Britain. The name Brighton was officially adopted by the town commissioners in 1810.

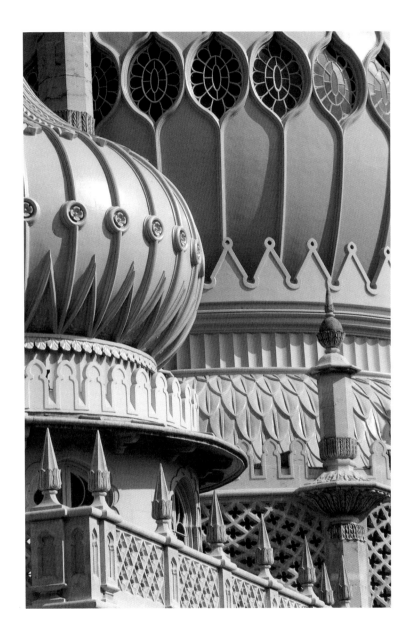

From the late eighteenth century as the town's population accelerated, urban development started to expand over the surrounding open farmland and along the coast. To cater for the new wealthy visitors and residents many of the outstanding Regency squares and terraces that give Brighton & Hove much of its architectural charm were constructed. Chichester Terrace (above) designed by the architect/builder partnership of Amon Wilds and Charles Busby formed part of what was to become one of the grandest urban compositions in England at Kemp Town on the resort's eastern fringe. The façades were completed in 1828 and the interiors fitted out by each owner to their particular taste.

Royal Crescent on the Marine Parade was built between 1798 and 1807 and with its black mathematical tiling was later described as 'the earliest unified composition of Brighton'. *(Below)* Brunswick Terrace, again completed in 1828, overlooking the lawns and promenade of Hove and built initially as part of the self-contained Brunswick Estate.

Another unified development, Regency Square was started in 1818 characterised by curving bow windows and ornate verandas – an architectural form later seen in many parts of the city. *(Right)* Adelaide Crescent, Hove, completed from 1834 onwards and notable for its sweeping curves merging into Palmeira Square.

Brunswick Square, along with Brunswick Terrace as part of the Brunswick Estate, was also designed by the Wilds/Busby partnership. When built the estate was known as Brunswick Town and complete with its own church, town hall and closed market. Mews were built behind for coaches and horses and also smaller housing for the estate's employees. The square is now regarded as one of the finest Regency examples in Britain, the cream painted houses with their bowed fronts and Ionic columns displaying a harmony and calm from a different age.

The Lanes. As Brighton expanded into its new role as a seaside resort and the fishing industry declined, the old part of the town became an increasingly poor district. It was not until the dawn of the twentieth century that its charm began to be appreciated and slowly many of the old cramped fishermen's and tradesmen's cottages and businesses were converted into the numerous small shops that today give The Lanes their distinctive and colourful character.

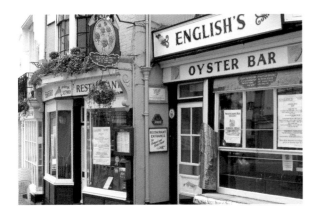

Although most of the premises probably only dated back to the eighteenth century, they represented in design and scale a medieval town. With their dense network of narrow and winding streets, alleys and footways interspersed by small squares, the district has now become one of the most picturesque in Brighton and a world famous tourist attraction.

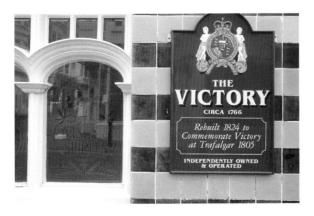

Looking down onto the lower promenade from King's Road with Brighton Pier in the distance. This stretch of beach adjacent to the old town was the area used for hauling fishing boats onto the shingle since no harbour has ever existed in Brighton. It was also used by sea bathers from the 1730s and increasingly after publication of Dr Richard Russell's dissertation referred to earlier. The cast iron railings and the King's Road arches below date from 1854 when the upper promenade was widened as far as the Hove boundary.

Brighton Pier at dusk. Seaside piers were constructed initially to serve packet boats and pleasure steamers but soon became popular with promenaders, enabling them to 'walk the waters' without any danger. Brighton Pier, previously known as the Palace Pier, was the third to be built in the town (after The Chain and West Piers), opening in 1899 and described as 'the grandest pier ever built'. Its pleasure facilities included shops, theatre and concert hall. Despite the many changes that have been made over the years, this 'palace of fun' is still one of the resort's principal attractions. Piers were also built at Bognor Regis, Eastbourne, Hastings and Worthing.

Brighton Rock in its many colours.

Opposite: A glorious early summer's day. The beach, blue skies, sun hats, coloured umbrellas, cold drinks, entertainment, striped deck chairs – everything one could wish for of an English seaside resort. The recently landscaped lower promenade has been an outstanding improvement to the seafront and now features numerous cafés, restaurants, pubs, clubs, galleries and games facilities. Most have seating outside enabling all to soak up the sunshine and seaside ambience. Only the fire-blackened, skeletal remains of the old West Pier in the background mar the scene.

(This page and opposite)
Colour at Brighton & Hove.

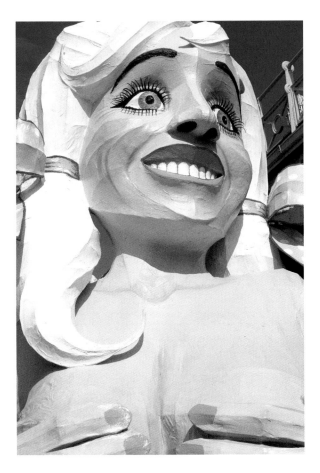

Spring at Palmeira Lawns, Hove. This fine square, at the eastern end of Hove is beautifully enhanced by its floral clock and surround-ing Victorian buildings. The flint church of St John the Baptist complements the scene and was built in the 1850s to cater for the rapidly growing population of this area. In St Ann's Gardens nearby is St Ann's Well, a chalybeate spring where water still flows. Once known as the Chalybeate Spa, its water was considered to have health-giving properties in the mid eighteenth century.

Brighton Marina. In 1963 a massive combined marina and residential and entertainment complex was proposed which, after much controversy and numerous planning difficulties, was finally opened by HM The Queen in 1979 below the cliffs just east of Kemp Town near Black Rock. The marina, the largest in Britain, consists of two enormous breakwaters enclosing an area in excess of 50 hectares and with moorings for some 2000 boats. The extensive marina village was delayed until 1985 due to financial and ownership problems. Now almost complete and with its many shops, designer outlets, restaurants, pubs, cinema, bowling centre, hotel and superstore the entire complex is proving to be an outstanding addition to the city.

Cyclists taking part in the annual London to Brighton cycle ride pass the finishing line on Madeira Drive. First held in 1975 the event now attracts over 27,000 participants each year cycling in aid of a major charity. Starting at half-hourly intervals, the fast enthusiastic riders often reach the resort for breakfast whilst the vast majority of entrants pedal more wearily to the finish throughout the remainder of the day. Other notable annual London to Brighton events include the famous veteran car run (old Crock's race) dating back to 1896, the Pioneer Motorcycle run started in 1937 and the Commercial Vehicle run.

Scenes and details from the 2007 Commercial Vehicle run on Madeira Drive.

Aspects of Shoreham-by-Sea. *(Top left)* Part of the Shoreham redoubt constructed in 1857 commanding the entrance to the harbour. Although much has been demolished, its defensive walls, caponniers and emplacements have been restored and are now classified as an ancient monument. *(Top right)* A painted mural features a London, Brighton and South Coast Railway carriage of the type once found here. *(Above)* The striking and unusual chequered stone and flint frontage to the twelfth century Marlipins, one of the few remaining buildings from New Shoreham's heyday. *(Left)* A plaque dedicated to Captain Henry Roberts who explored the South Seas with Captain Cook.

Afternoon calm, Shoreham Harbour. The navigable River Adur flows down from the Sussex Weald to reach the sea at Shoreham west of Hove. Prior to 1100 Shoreham's port was situated about 5km upstream from the present harbour on the east bank of the river but due to severe silting after that date, a town known as New Shoreham was founded near the river's mouth, superseding the old port which reverted back to a small village simply known as Old Shoreham. New Shoreham prospered well into the fourteenth century as one of the most important towns in the south until it too was drastically affected by further silting and changes to the river's course, the sea then destroying much of the town. It was mainly the rapid growth of nearby Brighton and Hove which led to an eventual cutting of a new river mouth through shingle banks in 1818 that revived Shoreham's importance and stabilised the river's movements, the town finally becoming known as Shoreham-by-Sea. The old water course parallel to the coast and originally directed towards Hove was then converted into a small harbour by the use of lock gates enabling vessels to berth at all stages of the tide. It is this that over the years has grown to become one of the busiest small ports in the country.

Old Shoreham. The original port's significance can now only be ascertained from the size and beauty of Old Shoreham's surviving part-Saxon Church of St Nicholas possibly dating back to about 900AD. The photograph shows a section of the church's later magnificent Norman tower.

A Bohemian heritage. At the head of a creek opposite the present town, rows of assorted houseboats line the water's edge of the spit known as Shoreham Beach. Lovingly created, some are simply domestic conversions of river or sea-going vessels, others are made up of redundant barges sometimes fitted out with unusual superstructures such as the coach shown here. Often known as 'Bungalow Town', Shoreham Beach once a popular theatre and film colony, at one time featured numerous somewhat ramshackle homes and holiday retreats improvised from old railway carriage bodies, tramcars or buses. Very few of these now remain and to a certain degree the area has lost part of its unique character.

Shoreham (Brighton City) Airport is situated on the west bank of the Adur opposite the site of Old Shoreham and just over 1km inland from the sea. With its single tarmacadam and three grass runways and opened in 1911, it is the oldest established airport in the UK and now a major base for corporate business aviation. Completed in 1936 the airport's Art Deco Grade II listed terminal building is a unique feature and still in everyday use by business, training and pleasure flyers alike including many visitors from Europe. Over the years the airport has seen both domestic and international flight usage by some of the world's largest airlines. Today guided tours, viewing areas and an airport archive and visitor centre are all available and an extensive programme of special events is held throughout the year.

The estuary of the River Adur adjacent to Old Shoreham. In the foreground the rotting spars and planking of possibly an old sailing barge hint at the river's former importance. Before the Romans arrived in Sussex, the Adur spread in a wide estuary as far as 10km inland to Steyning and Upper Beeding, both heavily reliant on waterborne trade. Steyning was once known as St Cuthman's Port after a local saint and its connections with the river. Behind the barge's remains the wooden trestle toll bridge of 1781, and now a footbridge, acted as an important link in the Sussex coastal road network. Lancing Chapel lies beyond on its hilltop site.

Clearing skies, Worthing. The beach, completely empty, dries out after a night's rain. Worthing Pier is in the background. Once a small fishing village, Worthing began to grow from the early years of the nineteenth century in a similar manner to Brighton having also been visited by royalty, in this case by Princess Amelia sister of the future Prince Regent. Initially the growth was somewhat spasmodic, partly due to the varying sanitary problems created by the flat landform and subsequent outbreaks of cholera and typhoid. By the twentieth century with these matters resolved the town quickly expanded to become the fourth largest in Sussex and with its 8km promenade, pier and part sandy beaches is now one of the most popular resorts along the coast. Small colourful boats and stalls at the shingle's edge scattered along the entire sea front from Lancing to Goring are evidence of the degree of fishing still carried out.

WORTHING to ALDWICK

A Worthing souvenir sweat shirt design.

Worthing to Aldwick features the last of the more conventional Sussex coastline before the watery reaches of Selsey, Pagham and Chichester Harbours. Behind the sea the flat, richly fertile coastal plain commencing at Lancing broadens out in an increasing manner to the southern slopes of the South Downs. Almost along this entire shore the beaches are of shingle with exposed sand at low tide and again with a history and evidence of erosion and tidal fluctuations. There are no cliffs, the absence of which has allowed the often considerable and haphazard urban development from villages and towns to penetrate to the shingle's edge.

Spectators line the world-class bowling greens at Worthing's Beach House Park during the National Bowls Championships held annually in the town.

Opposite: The view looking east from the pier across deserted sands at low tide on a stormy winter's afternoon towards distant Lancing and Shoreham-by-Sea.

The traditional pleasure cruise ship *Balmoral* berthed at the pier takes on holiday makers bound for a day's cruise to the Isle of Wight and Dorset's Jurassic coast. *Balmoral* together with the historic *Waverley*, the last sea-going paddle steamer in the world, are regular visitors to the south coast, their annual summer programme organised by Waverley Excursions featuring numerous day trips from many southern ports including Bournemouth, Portsmouth, Southampton, Swanage, Weymouth and the Isle of Wight.

Huge piles of washed-up timber on the beach await collection and disposal in late January 2008. The timber was lost from the cargo ship *Ice Prince* sunk some 25 nautical miles off the Dorset coast whilst carrying 5000 tonnes of the wood to Greece. Much of the vessel's cargo ended up scattered along many of the Sussex beaches, Worthing being the most badly affected. The scale of the hazard made national news headlines providing Worthing with an influx of visitors and sightseers normally unknown in January. Sailors and watersports enthusiasts were urged to take extreme care from the danger of collision with the often large sections of floating timber.

Seaside architecture at Heene Terrace, Marine Parade and Ambrose Place.

High Salvington Post Mill. The black weatherboarded mill on the northern outskirts of Worthing dates from about 1720 and after cessation of working in 1897 and a long period of neglect, restoration was commenced in 1976. Now fully operational it is one of the last surviving examples of a post mill in Sussex, the main mill structure being suspended on a post around which it turns to face the wind.

Misericords, the Church of St Andrew, West Tarring. It is relatively unusual to find misericords in parish churches but there are six in this thirteenth-century church all backing on to the fifteenth-century screen and facing the altar. Misericords are simply wooden brackets below the underside of hinged choir stall seats. When the seat is raised they then act as a support for the occupant when standing. In their semi-hidden environment they attracted meticulous attention from their carvers, often encouraging a remarkable freedom of expression, every misericord bearing a different design. An example from the church is shown here. Tarring village, now engulfed by the main town, is also noted for its attractive curving High Street, its parish hall, once being a Palace of the Archbishops of Canterbury and its unusual orchards of fig trees.

Part of the unique painted ceiling within the English Martyrs' Church at Goring. Carried out solely by Gary Bevans over a five-and-a-half year period with full support from the church authorities, the ceiling is an exact copy of the restored ceiling in the Sistine Chapel in Rome, painted by Michaelangelo. The colours were made to match the original and the final artwork has been reduced to about two-thirds scale. Completed in 1993 the ceiling is an amazing example of one person's religious inspiration.

Vegetated shingle at Kingston Gorse near Ferring. Whilst not a common coastal sight, there are several areas along the Sussex shore where the shingle beaches support a variety of plant species notably at Rye Harbour, Shoreham Beach, here, Aldwick and Pagham. Plants such as Sea Holly, Yellow-horned Poppy and Sea Kale with their long root systems clearly thrive on such a barren, dry habitat despite the often windy or sunny conditions prevailing. It is claimed that rocks visible off shore at low tide are the remains of Kingston Chapel destroyed by the sea's encroachment in the seventeenth century. Evidence of this encroachment can be seen along much of this particular coastline where truncated lanes and byways point mysteriously out to sea to the drowned communities of Charlton, Ilsham, Cudlowe and others lost over the centuries.

Opposite: Beach huts and fish boxes add colour to the shingle at Goring-by-Sea. The famous natural history writer Richard Jefferies lived his last years in Goring and the village is particularly noted for its one mile long avenue of evergreen Holm Oak trees linking it with nearby Ferring. From the top of Highdown Hill, some 4 km to the north on the edge of the Downs, one can, on a clear day, see almost the entire length of the Sussex coast from Selsey Bill to beyond Beachy Head.

The painted sign outside the Steam Packet Inn at Littlehampton gives a hint of the town's former maritime history. Littlehampton's importance grew as it succeeded inland Arundel as the major port on the River Arun with the construction of new quays and improved harbour entrance in the mid eighteenth century capable of taking larger vessels. Becoming a popular seaside resort some 100 years later, it was frequented by numerous writers and artists including Byron, Samuel Taylor Coleridge, Leader and Constable. Described by Pevsner as 'pleasant but exasperatingly disjointed', the town grew up in a piecemeal fashion mainly along the river's east bank a short distance from the sea with further detached terracing nearer the coast. Both parts were later linked by infilling during the latter half of the nineteenth and early twentieth centuries. In recent years as trade has declined the harbour's facilities have been steadily reduced, fortunately to be replaced by major regeneration of the old quays with waterside homes, riverside walks, pubs, cafés and restaurants bringing an air of vibrancy back to the town.

Looking across Littlehampton Harbour and new marina to the east bank with its recent waterside development. A guide book from the early twentieth century noted the port's falling trade when it described 'at the western end of the esplanade is the harbour which with its antiquated wharves and tall-masted ships is a never failing source of interest to visitors, notwithstanding the inferiority of its trade to that of bygone days'. Until 1882 cross-channel passenger steamers were operated regularly from Littlehampton to the Channel Islands and France in conjunction with the London, Brighton & South Coast Railway.

Arundel Castle. Arundel Castle, the ancestral home of the Dukes of Norfolk, with its multitude of round and square towers overlooking the ancient town dates from an almost total rebuilding between 1890 and 1903. Fragments of the original Norman Castle, ruined during the Civil War, still remain including the keep and barbican. Rebuilt in a Gothic style and on a grandiose scale not dissimilar to Windsor Castle, it is impressive not only for its location but for its sheer size.

A wintry late afternoon with the silhouette of the castle viewed from the hills behind and with light on the distant sea near Littlehampton. The town itself some 5km inland from Littlehampton is situated mainly on a ridge sloping down to the River Arun where the Downs meet the coastal plain and where signs of the town's past history as a port can still be seen. From the south Arundel has one of the most dramatic skylines in England being dominated by its castle, cathedral and parish church with period close-knit housing stepping down to the water's edge. The town has become a major centre for the antiques trade and the venue for the annual Arundel Arts Festival.

The Church of St Andrew-by-the-Ford, Ford. The solitary eleventh-century church stands close to the River Arun between Arundel and Littlehampton out on the windswept coastal plain with the South Downs on the skyline. Ian Nairn in *The Buildings of England* describes it as 'one of Sussex's prettiest churches' with 'a lovable unrestored interior, nave and chancel, brick porch and white painted bellcote in a small churchyard almost surrounded by large trees'. Isolated in the fields and once used as a navigation beacon by river shipping, the church is situated near the site of the river's junction with the old Portsmouth to Arundel canal which ceased commercial use in the mid nineteenth century.

Norman doorways. Also on the coastal plain, practically within sound of the sea and less than 2km from St Andrew's Church at Ford, lie two other well-known Sussex churches both of which contain considerable evidence of their Norman history, particularly by the rich decoration and mouldings to their entrance doorways. *(Above)* The Church of St Thomas, Tortington, additionally known for the unique 'beakhead' carvings to its chancel arch. *(Right)* The Church of St Mary, Climping, its doorway carvings regarded as the finest in Sussex. A saying for West Sussex churches describes 'Climping for perfection'.

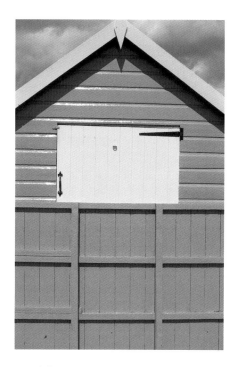  

Beach huts, Felpham. Immediately east of Bognor Regis, the village of Felpham still contains considerable interest with its flint walls, cottages, trees and medieval church. William Blake, poet, painter and mystic lived here in the early nineteenth century encouraged by the poet and biographer William Hayley. Blake wrote of Felpham:

> Away to sweet Felpham for heaven is there;
> The ladder of Angels descends through the air
> On the turret its spiral does softly descend
> Through the village it winds, at my cot it does end.

Whether Blake would write similar words of Felpham now is of course debatable but for many its seafront extending to Bognor's promenade is still a great place for a stroll at any time of day or simply watching the world go by. Its colour is strikingly enhanced by the rows of brightly decorated beach huts.

The pier, Bognor Regis. Described as the most westerly of the classic Sussex coast 'watering places' the name Bognor Regis is loosely used now to include the hamlets or villages of Aldwick, the Bersteds, Elmer, Felpham, Flansham and Middleton all absorbed into one large urban composition. Despite earlier schemes Bognor did not develop until after the 1820's again in imitation of the larger seaside resorts and like Littlehampton in a remarkably piecemeal fashion. Contemporary accounts refer to its 'professed design of making Bognor the resort of more select company than is to be found at other bathing places' and perhaps its earlier somewhat fragmented plan of housing achieved this. It has always been regarded as quiet and unpretentious, factors that have no doubt encouraged its numerous visitors and in particular King George V for convalescence in 1929 following which the town was granted the title of 'Regis'. Bognor's pier was built in 1865 followed over the years with various additions and alterations but its length was later severely curtailed by storm damage in the 1960s and 1999.

A colourful seafront corner of Bognor Regis.

Opposite: Butlin's Holiday Resort. Despite its multiplicity of building styles including such classic Regency examples as The Steyne, its Bath House, the Royal Norfolk Hotel, Russell Place, Hotham Park House or Hothampton Crescent, Bognor's best known building is surely the huge white undulating dome at Butlin's Holiday Resort. With its sweeping, flowing curves, the building is often visible over great distances particularly in sunlight when its light surface acts as an enormous reflector. There has been a Butlin's holiday camp in the town since 1960, a factor which undoubtedly has increased Bognor's visitor numbers and promoted its seaside attractions and after a recent multi-million pound make-over, Butlin's is still as popular as ever. For the town's residents the question has always been asked as to whether the high security fencing surrounding Butlin's is simply to keep its visitors inside or the residents outside!

Crowds enjoy the international Bognor Birdman Event. Of all the special weekend events held in the various Sussex coast resorts, Bognor's Birdman competition must be one of the most unusual. First held in the town in 1978, the aim of the charitable event is to provide a challenge of unpowered flight for competitors willing to launch themselves over the sea from Bognor's pier. Flyers are categorised for either self/team design and build innovative craft or modified hang glider and similar craft. Awards are given for longest time in the air, distance flown and most entertaining or comic entrant. The ultimate challenge is to exceed a 100m flight. With considerable secondary entertainment around the town, the two day event now attracts thousands of onlookers and is rightly featured as one of the resort's highlights of the year.

A winter sunset over Bognor Pier.

For many, Aldwick on the west flank of Bognor Regis, is a place of both municipal and private estates featuring homes of varying degrees of opulence and style. In particular the Aldwick Bay Estate is notable for its standards of buildings and quality of design. Once dubbed The Sussex Riviera, its 1920s' brochure proclaimed the estates 'nice type of seaside residences', and 'its peaceful neighbourhood not invaded by trippers and charabanc parties'! For others the quiet peaceful beach is also an attraction, one of its more unusual features being these remains of a wartime floating concrete 'Mulberry' harbour pontoon intended for use in France during the D-Day invasion by Allied forces and probably assembled at Selsey.

The peace and quiet of Aldwick

Pagham Harbour is one of the few totally undeveloped areas of the coast in West Sussex. The open landscape still retains a sense of wilderness and is extremely popular with ornithologists, being reclaimed for agriculture in the late nineteenth century only to flood again during storms in the early twentieth century. The harbour and surrounding pasture are of international importance for wintering wildfowl and wading birds. As a local nature reserve extending to some 600ha, the area encompasses a variety of habitats including salt marsh and mudflats intermingled with shingle beaches, reed beds and wet grassland. The photograph looks east across the harbour at high tide towards the distant village of Pagham itself.

PAGHAM to THORNEY

An exhibition of paintings in the Pagham Harbour Visitor Centre.

On this final section of a Sussex coastal journey, both the shoreline and the inland scenery change entirely. The predominant feature is the inter-tidal waters of both Pagham and Chichester harbours, the latter with its numerous, sometimes winding navigable channels and a haven for recreational sailing. Between the harbours, the low-lying Manhood Peninsula broadens south from Chichester to Selsey Bill, the most southerly point in Sussex, a landscape of rich fertile farmland open to wide skies and with a character more attributable to Lincolnshire than West Sussex. With fields and hedgerows often extending to the harbour's tree-lined banks, there is little urban development apart from Selsey and the Witterings where the award-winning sands act as a magnet for sun worshippers.

Behind the curving shoreline and Pagham Harbour, the Manhood Peninsula being almost entirely flat is drained by a network of rifes and ditches interspersed by isolated, often medieval farms and hamlets and narrow tortuous lanes. Despite its close proximity to the city of Chichester, it is still in places relatively unknown to many people. This view shows Pagham Rife, one of the principal drainage outlets for the peninsula and for the recently completed Chichester flood relief scheme, near North Honer Farm with its willow-lined banks in early summer.

A crop of pumpkins ripen under late summer skies near Honer.

A bleak winter scene looking over the harbour and the outlet of the Pagham Rife after a scattering of snow. At one time heavy snowfalls were common in Sussex particularly on the Downs and towards the county's eastern boundary with Kent. In recent years, however, it has been highly unusual to find any amount of snow laying on the southern fringes of the coastal plain and especially on Pagham Harbour's salt marshes.

Opposite: The view looking north from the strengthened Pagham Harbour wall across the fields of Honer and South Mundham to the distant South Downs. Nearby Bowley Farm House, dating back to the thirteenth century is reputedly where Thomas A'Beckett and Henry II met.

St Wilfred's Chapel at Church Norton lies on the western shore of Pagham Harbour just inland from the sea. The chapel is all that remains of Selsey's former parish church, which was removed from Church Norton to its present-day site in Selsey in the nineteenth century, leaving only the chancel. It dates from the thirteenth century and it has been speculated that the original church may have been built on or near the site of St Wilfred's cathedral church lost to the sea. There were twenty three Bishops of Selsey between 709 and 1070, before the bishopric was transferred to Chichester. Earthworks surrounding the churchyard are thought to have originated from a small Norman castle built to defend the once navigable harbour.

Sunset over Pagham Harbour looking west to Church Norton and St Wilfred's Chapel.

Taking advantage of the fertile soils and high quality of light in this region, many crops are grown in an extremely intensive manner. This view shows young lettuce plants in fields near Selsey.

Left: A Selsey Heritage Trail plaque tells of these fields' former use in darker days. Due to the flat nature of the land many small airstrips were built in the Second World War as satellite fields to the well-known Tangmere airbase east of Chichester.

Selsey, meaning Seal Island, was once an island at the tip of the Manhood Peninsula an area notorious for its coastal erosion, dangerous currents and treacherous sandbanks. It is said that the village has lost over 2km of land to the sea since Domesday. Fishing has always been a major occupation with cockles, prawns, lobsters, crabs and oysters once extensively caught but in more recent times, having grown as a dormitory town to Chichester, it has also taken on the status of a small seaside holiday resort. The photograph shows Selsey's eastern shoreline with its essential lifeboat station responsible for the saving of hundred of lives over the years in these uncertain waters.

Windsurfers at Bracklesham Bay. A short distance west of Selsey, Bracklesham Bay and East Wittering merge to form a small but popular resort famed for its broad sands at low tide and as a shore to find fossils, particularly sharks' teeth, dating back millions of years.

Seaside art and architecture, East Wittering.

(Above) Redundant railway carriages form the basis of an inter-war years bungalow of the type once common at Shoreham Beach, Lancing, Pagham and East Wittering.

Behind the ever eroding coast that extends between Selsey and Bracklesham, the western half of the Manhood Peninsula stretches away to the Downs. Near Ham Farm only 1km inland from the bleak shingle, geological evidence can still be found of Selsey's history as an island, a situation that could re-occur at some future date. In spring the rich farmland can be a blaze of colour, as shown here, echoing to the continual chorus of skylarks.

A rounded flint cobbled barn at Easton Farm near Bracklesham acts as a reminder of the area's considerable fertility.

Patriotic colours at West Wittering. The unspoilt sandy beach at West Wittering close to the entrance to Chichester Harbour has been popular with bathers for many years and more recently with windsurfers. Often classified as one of the best beaches in the UK, it has regularly received clean beach and water quality awards.

A crowded scene on West Wittering beach on a hot summer's afternoon. Because of the popularity of this beach it is not uncommon to find traffic queues in high summer extending the entire length of the Manhood Peninsula from the Witterings to the Chichester By-pass and beyond.

'Summertime' at Chichester Yacht Basin. Chichester Harbour extends to some 30 sq km of inter-tidal waters and almost 30 km of navigable channels. Between the seventeenth and nineteenth centuries it was a busy commercial harbour but today it is used solely for recreational sailing with several marinas, sailing clubs and associations, sailing schools, activity centres and boatyards. Cruises are available for visitors wishing to tour the harbour and view its wildlife. Chichester Yacht Basin is often host to several thousand craft at any one time and is shown here on a crowded day.

Opposite: West Wittering beach sweeps north into Chichester Harbour at East Head, an area of quickly changing tides and light, wide indented sands and for most of the year generally devoid of human presence. East Head Spit, projecting into the harbour, is at present in considerable danger of being washed away, its sand-dunes and marram grass under constant attack by the eroding waters. Although protection measures have been undertaken, there is much concern about the consequences to the harbour itself should the spit be destroyed. The photograph shows the empty beach at low tide near East Head. The Isle of Wight can be seen in the far distance with Hayling Island on the right of the picture.

Aspects of Chichester Harbour. It is now considered likely that the harbour was one of the sites for the Roman invasion of Britain. Certainly many of the attractive villages and hamlets along its waters have names derived from Saxon origins, indicating the importance and history of this popular area.

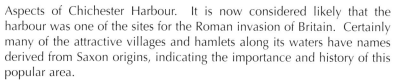

For nearly 100 years the city of Chichester, county town of West Sussex and classified as an inland port was linked to the harbour near Birdham by the Portsmouth to Arundel Canal and its short connecting arm to Chichester Basin. Finally closed in 1906, much of the waterway between the city and the harbour has in recent years been dredged and cleared, being developed as a recreational and leisure amenity by the Chichester Canal Society whose ultimate aim is to restore navigation between the two centres. This view shows one of the society's vessels near Hunston not far from where JMW Turner painted his famous view of Chichester Cathedral in 1830.

Daybreak at Dell Quay. During the middle ages prior to the building of the canal, cargoes and merchandise for Chichester were shipped to Dell Quay and then transferred by wagon to the city. Dell Quay was therefore a major factor in the city's growth and prosperity. Sailing is now the main activity from the quay which is also the location for the Chichester Harbour Conservancy's Education Centre hosting numerous lectures, demonstrations, activities and walks throughout the year. The photograph illustrates the harbour looking south from Dell Quay towards Birdham and Itchenor in early morning light.

A few stones are all that survive of the foundations to the tidal salt mill which stood at the entrance to the millpond in Fishbourne Creek, captured here on a still, misty morning. A causeway, which was part of the mill pond embankment leads out to it. Fishbourne had, at one time during the nineteenth century, three mills and a windmill, salt production being an important industry in Chichester Harbour.

The remains of a hypocaust or under-floor heating system at Fishbourne Roman Palace. At the head of the harbour the largest known Roman domestic building north of the Alps was discovered in 1961 at Fishbourne. Within the foundations of the four-winged palace were the remains of more than twenty mosaic floors, many complete with their own under-floor heating systems. The site now fully protected and including a Roman plant display area, has become a leading museum receiving several million visitors since its opening to the public in 1968. The palace is further evidence of the possibility of the harbour acting as a site for the Roman invasion of Britain.

A grey cold mist hangs over the stillness of Chichester Harbour at Cutmill Creek. Bosham Church can be seen in the distance. The mill which once stood near this site ceased working in the early 1920s.

(Opposite) Looking across to Bosham on a calm still winter's morning. The village of Bosham at the head of the harbour's Bosham Channel was an important Saxon settlement and the tower of the beautiful Holy Trinity Church, with its outstanding chancel arch, dates from this period. The church appears on the Bayeaux Tapestry in connection with Harold's ill-fated visit to Normandy in 1064, two years before the Norman invasion. The village has been known for centuries for its shipbuilding and as a fishing community, but now generally regarded as the most attractive village around the harbour, it is a popular tourist and sailing haunt.

Bosham Quay and the Raptackle on a late winter's afternoon. Legend has it that it was at Bosham that King Canute sat in his chair and attempted to command the tide to retreat. The discovery of a child's tomb in the church during the Victorian period led to further speculation that it might have been that of Canute's daughter.

Sunset over the still waters of Bosham Channel at high tide.

Towards the end of a coastal journey – sunset over Chichester Harbour viewed from Cobnor Point on the tip of the Chidham peninsula. At the end of the eighteenth century a variety of wheat, known as Chidham wheat, was discovered here and became famous for its prolific yield of grain. A crop is still grown at the Weald and Downland Open Air Museum north of Chichester.

1939 – 1945

IN MEMORY
OF THOSE
WHO GAVE
THEIR LIVES FOR
THEIR COUNTRY

ZUR ERINNERUNG
AN DIE, DIE DAS
LEBEN FÜR
DAS VATERLAND
GEOPFERT HABEN

Thorney Island. The name Thorney is derived from the Saxon the 'thorn tree island'. Separated from the mainland by the Little Deep and the Great Deep, but to all appearances a peninsula, Thorney was from 1938 to 1976 an important RAF base, later becoming a settlement station for Vietnamese refugees and then a base for the Royal Artillery. In the graveyard of the twelfth century Church of St Nicholas at West Thorney, gravestones commemorate both Allied and German pilots who lost their lives during the Second World War. In this quiet, remote, peaceful location a short distance from the waters of Hampshire and the Emsworth Channel, we have reached the end of a coastal journey and the end of all things.

ACKNOWLEDGEMENTS

Once again I would like to thank those people who have helped me in the compilation of this book by allowing photography, providing information and for advising on or contributing to captions and text. In particular I am most grateful to the following:

Jean Barnes for allowing the use of the late Tony Barnes' image on page 96; the Reverend Bernard Crosby and John Taylor for information provided on St Nicholas Chapel of Ease, Pett Level; Joy Whiting; The Management and Staff at Chichester Harbour Conservancy, De la Warr Pavilion, English Martyrs Church - Goring, The National Trust and The Friends of the High Salvington Mill.

As always special thanks go to Joy for her infinite patience, support and hard work in typing the manuscript and finally, of course, to Steven Pugsley and his enthusiastic colleagues at Halsgrove for their faith and assistance.

REFERENCE SOURCES

There are numerous books, booklets, papers, leaflets and guides about Sussex and its coastline.
It is an impossible task to mention them all but the following have been invaluable as reference sources:

Arscott, D *Curiosities of West Sussex* SB Publications, 1993
AA Illustrated Guide to Britain Drive Publications, 1974
Barnes, J, Barnes, T and Whiting, J *Misericords in Sussex* The University of Chichester 2007
Brandon, P *Sussex* Robert Hale, 2006
Brandon, P *The Sussex Landscape* Hodder & Stoughton, 1974
------ *Bognor Regis* Bognor Regis Local History Society, 1981
Bridgewater, P *An eccentric tour of Sussex* Snake River Press, 2007
Collins, S *A Sussex Miscellany* Snake River Press, 2007
George, M *The South Downs* Pavilion, 1992
Godwin, J *The Military Defence of West Sussex* Middleton Press, 1985
Harries, D *Maritime Sussex* SB publications, 1997
Leslie, K *A Sense of Place* West Sussex County Council, 2006
Leslie, K and Short, B *An Historical Atlas of Sussex* Phillimore, 1999
Lloyd, D *Historic Towns of Kent and Sussex* Victor Gollancz, 1991
McGowan, I *A Portrait of Brighton & Hove* Halsgrove, 2004
McGowan, I *Moods of Sussex* Halsgrove, 2006
McGowan, I *Moods of the South Downs* Halsgrove 2007
McGowan, I and Hole, J *Mundham & Runcton* MMMBC, 2000
McGowan, I and Pailthorpe, R *Chichester, A Contemporary View* John Wiley, 1994
McGowan, I and Pailthorpe, R *Chichester, A Millennium View* John Wiley, 2000
Mee, A *The Kings England: Sussex* Hodder & Stoughton, 1964
Mitchell, W *East Sussex – A Shell guide* Faber & Faber, 1978
Nairn, I and Pevsner, N *The Buildings of England: Sussex* Penguin Books, 1975
Roger, J *Chichester Harbour* Phillimore, 1996
Somerville, C and Bethell, J *English Harbours and Coastal Villages* Weidenfeld and Nicholson, 1989
Swinfen, W and Arscott, D *Hidden Sussex* BBC Radio Sussex, 1984
Talbot, R and Whiteman, R *England* Cassell, 2000
Talbot, R and Whiteman, R *The Garden of England* Weidenfeld & Nicholson, 1995
Wales, T *The West Sussex Village Book* Countryside Books, 1984

Guides and leaflets to the many attractions, museums, places of interest and churches featured within this book.